To Tommy

Enjoy the story,
remember the message.
Read Always

Love You Still

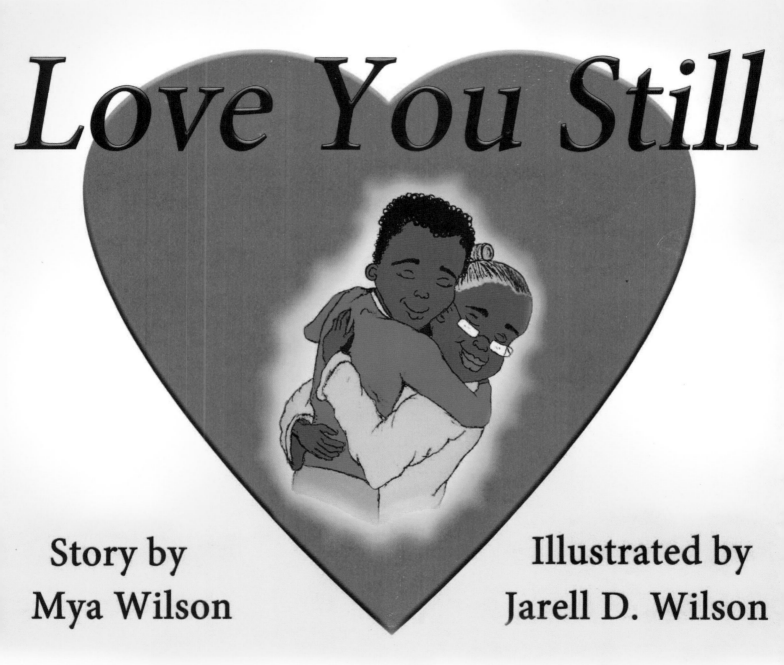

Story by
Mya Wilson

Illustrated by
Jarell D. Wilson

Printed in the United States of America

Published by:
Cousin Connections Publishing
40 West 116th Street
New York, NY 10026

ISBN: 978-1519516572

Printed by Create Space

Dedicated to...

Our grandmother whose artistic talent we've inherited
-MW and JDW

All of the children that call me "Auntie Mya"
and to every student I have ever taught
-MW

My nieces and nephew who I will always love and hope to inspire
-JDW

Sometimes grown ups get mad and frown
up their faces at the things you do.
They might even yell and holler too.

But did you know?...
They always will...
love you still.

When you do something that you're not supposed to...
Your mom may say she is disappointed in you.

It was just an accident when you broke your dad's new tool.

But you were only playing with it because you thought it was cool.

Dad may seem really angry with you...
But did you know?...

Dad always will...

love you *still*.

Your older sister really hates,
when you hold her up and make her late.

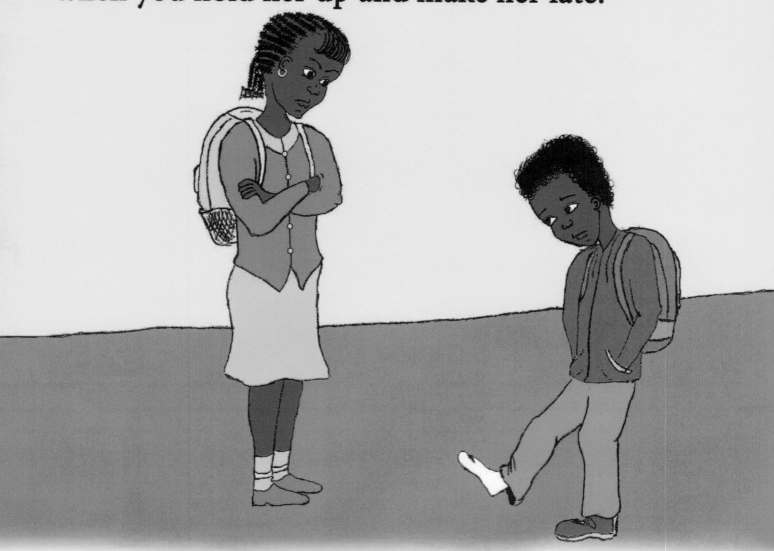

Making her late is what you often do,

but you were only trying to find your other shoe.

But did you know?...
Your sister always will...

love you still.

Your older brother got really mad at you, when you spilled juice on his favorite shirt. He even called you names like "doofus" or "twirp".

Grandma may get upset,
when you rush through your homework
and it looks a sloppy mess.

You knew that it wasn't your very best.

Although Grandma is tired and stressed

Did you know?...Grandma always will...*love you still.*

Sometimes you and your classmates misbehave in school...

and act like you all have forgotten every rule.

There will be lots of times when the things you do will upset the family members and the grown ups around you.

But it's very important for you to know...

No matter how disappointed, angry or upset they may be...

Mya and Jarell are first cousins and have been close since they were small. When they were young they planned to create a comic book together. This is their first collaboration. They hope to create more amazing children's stories.

About the author

Mya Wilson was raised in Harlem, New York and is currently a teacher in New York City. She has been teaching for many years, and enjoys reading to her students more than anything else. Mya also enjoys reading herself and creating things. Mya is a grade school teacher dedicated to helping small children discover their voice. She plans to write other children's books, and encourages all children to follow their dreams.

About the illustrator

Jarell D. Wilson was born and raised in Long Island, New York. Since his early years, Jarell has been drawing and finding ways to express his creativity through art. Throughout the years he has worked with children, from being a summer camp counselor to a foster care family specialist. He is grateful he can be a positive influence in the lives of children and hopes to continue that influence through his art. Jarell wants to help children find their outlet of creative expression and inspire them to share it with the world

Made in the USA
Charleston, SC
03 January 2016